DISASTER WARNING!

HURRICANES

by Rex Ruby

Consultant: Beth Gambro
Reading Specialist, Yorkville, Illinois

BEARPORT
PUBLISHING

Minneapolis, Minnesota

T0389975

Teaching Tips

Before Reading

- Look at the cover of the book. Discuss the picture and the title.
- Ask readers to brainstorm a list of what they already know about hurricanes. What can they expect to see in the book?
- Go on a picture walk, looking through the pictures to discuss vocabulary and make predictions about the text.

During Reading

- Read for purpose. Encourage readers to think about the kinds of things that might happen during a hurricane.
- Ask readers to look for the details of the book. What are the dangers of a hurricane?
- If readers encounter an unknown word, ask them to look at the sounds in the word. Then, ask them to look at the rest of the page. Are there any clues to help them understand?

After Reading

- Encourage readers to pick a buddy and reread the book together.
- Ask readers to name two ways to stay safe during a hurricane. Find the pages that tell about these things.
- Ask readers to write or draw something they learned about hurricanes.

Credits

Cover and title page, © FotoKina/Shutterstock; 3, © Den Rozhnovsky/Shutterstock and © BEST-BACKGROUNDS/Shutterstock; 5, © izanbar/iStock; 7, © FotoKina/Shutterstock; 8–9, © Bilanol/Shutterstock; 11, © Bilanol/Shutterstock; 12–13, © Ivan Ventura/Shutterstock; 14–15, © Bilanol/Shutterstock; 17, © Rokas/Adobe Stock; 19, © Zabavna/iStock; 21, © Chadolfski/Shutterstock; 22T, © Gizem Gecim/iStock; 22M, © FrankRamspott/iStock; 22B, © Carlos Flores/iStock; 23TL, © pisaphotography/Shutterstock; 23TM, © Bilanol/Shutterstock; 23TR, © ghornephoto/iStock; 23BL, © Bilanol/Shutterstock; 23BM, © Drew McArthur/Shutterstock; 23BR, © EHStockphoto/Shutterstock.

See BearportPublishing.com for our statement on Generative AI Usage.

Library of Congress Cataloging-in-Publication Data

Names: Ruby, Rex, author.
Title: Hurricanes / by Rex Ruby.
Description: Minneapolis, Minnesota : Bearport Publishing Company, [2026] | Series: Disaster warning! | "Bearcub books." | Includes bibliographical references and index.
Identifiers: LCCN 2024062286 (print) | LCCN 2024062287 (ebook) | ISBN 9798892329897 (library binding) | ISBN 9798895774205 (paperback) | ISBN 9798895771068 (ebook)
Subjects: LCSH: Hurricanes--Juvenile literature. | Meteorology--Juvenile literature.
Classification: LCC QC944.2 .R823 2026 (print) | LCC QC944.2 (ebook) | DDC 551.552--dc23/eng/20250212
LC record available at https://lccn.loc.gov/2024062286
LC ebook record available at https://lccn.loc.gov/2024062287

For more information, write to Bearport Publishing, 3500 American Blvd W, Suite 150, Bloomington, MN 55431.

Contents

Over the Ocean

Rain falls along the **coast**.

Trees bend from the strong winds.

Warning!

A **hurricane** is coming!

4

Say hurricane like HUR-uh-kane

5

A hurricane is a huge spinning storm.

It has lots of rain and very strong winds.

Whoosh!

Hurricanes form over the ocean.

Then, they may move onto land.

There, hurricanes can cause **disasters**.

9

Hurricane winds can knock over trees.

They may break windows.

The storms can even blow roofs off homes!

Hurricanes also push ocean water onto land.

This is called a storm surge.

Storm surges can cause **floods**.

13

Floods may cover streets.

The water can get into homes.

Sometimes, floods trap people inside.

15

How can you stay safe?

Check **weather reports**.

Hurricanes often take days to reach land.

This gives people time to find a safe place.

If a hurricane hits, stay inside.

Go into a small room.

Stay far away from windows.

Hurricanes can cause lots of **damage**.

But people come together to rebuild after the storm.

21

Hurricane Facts

The center of a hurricane is called the eye.

The eye

Hurricanes are given names. Some big hurricanes have been named Andrew, Rita, and Katrina.

Hurricane winds can knock out electricity.

Glossary

 **coast** land that runs along an ocean

 **damage** to cause harm

 **disasters** events that cause much damage or suffering

 **floods** lots of extra water that spreads over land

 **hurricane** a storm that forms over the ocean

 **weather reports** news on what the weather will be like

Index

Read More

London, Martha. *Windy Weather (What Is Weather?).* Minneapolis: Bearport Publishing Company, 2025.

Peterson, Megan Cooley. *How Does a Hurricane Form? (Science Questions).* Minneapolis: Jump! Inc., 2024.

Learn More Online

1. Go to **FactSurfer.com** or scan the QR code below.
2. Enter "**Hurricanes Warning**" into the search box.
3. Click on the cover of this book to see a list of websites.

About the Author

Rex Ruby lives in Minnesota with his family. Running against the wind is one of his favorite things to do.